13 13 4 4

D1516051

AN
EASY-READ
FACT
BOOK

Cats

Martyn Hamer

Franklin Watts

London   New York   Toronto   Sydney

© 1983 Franklin Watts Ltd

First published in Great Britain in
   1983 by
Franklin Watts Ltd
8 Cork Street
London W1

First published in the USA by
Franklin Watts Inc.
387 Park Avenue South
New York
N.Y. 10016

UK ISBN: 0 86313 013 5
US ISBN: 0-531-04510-2
Library of Congress Catalog Card
   Number: 82-51004

Printed in Great Britain by
   Cambus Litho, East Kilbride

Illustrated by
Christopher Forsey
Hayward Art Group

Designed and produced by
David Jefferis

Technical consultant
Peter Messent MA D.Phil
   of Pedigree Petfoods

AN
EASY-READ
FACT
BOOK

Contents

Prehistoric cats

Cats have lived on Earth for millions of years. The first cat-like animal was *Dinictis*, which lived about 36 million years ago.

The descendants of *Dinictis* developed in two ways. One branch became saber-tooths – big cats with huge tusk-like teeth. They died out about 30,000 years ago. The other branch of the cat family continues to flourish. The scientific name for this family is *Felidae*. Today there are many types of cat, from mighty tigers and lions to our small household animals. They are all members of the *Felidae* family.

Our household pets are probably descended from the African wildcat. This was first tamed by the peoples of Ancient Egypt, who used cats to keep grain stores free of the rats and mice which ate the food.

▷ Neanderthal men may have hunted Scimitar cats like this pair. Their skins would have made warm clothing for the prehistoric men. Scimitars died out about 30,000 years ago.

Goddess or devil?

△ A statue of Bast, the cat-goddess of pleasure. Once each year, a huge festival was held on the banks of the River Nile. Hundreds of thousands of people came to see the processions and join in the merrymaking which followed.

The Ancient Egyptians worshipped many different gods and goddesses, each of which ruled a part of daily life. Bast was the cat-goddess of pleasure, also thought to protect people from disease and evil spirits.

Killing a cat, even by accident, was a crime in Ancient Egypt. The punishment was death. The sacred animals were so highly worshipped that if a building caught fire, people were often

more concerned to rescue any cats trapped inside than to put out the fire.

When they died, cats were mummified and placed in temples. Nowadays many museums have examples of these cat mummies on display.

Other peoples have had quite different ideas about cats. To the Romans they were symbols of freedom. In the Europe of the Middle Ages, cats were thought to be agents of the devil.

△ In the Middle Ages, owning a cat, especially a black one, was a sure sign that you were a witch. Many people really thought that witches like this rode the night skies on their broomsticks.

Wildcats

△ There are two types of ocelot, both with dark stripes. This one is a Painted Ocelot, with a yellowish background. The Gray Ocelot is a reddish-gray color. Some people have tamed ocelots to keep them as beautiful pets.

Wildcats are very much like household cats in size and shape.

The Scottish wildcat, like the one snarling on the right, lives in the highlands of Scotland. It looks rather like an ordinary tabby but is more heavily built. It has thick fur, to keep out the cold, and a bushy blunt-tipped tail. Wildcats were hunted almost to extinction in the nineteenth century, but they are now on the increase again.

The ocelot comes from the forests of Central and South America. It has a beautiful coat which, sadly, is much in demand for clothing. Hunters have killed many ocelots and still do so. In the wild, ocelots live mostly in trees, feeding on birds, snakes and other small animals.

There are lots of other wildcats around the world, including bobcats, lynx, the margay, and wildcats from Africa and India.

▽ This Scottish wildcat lives mainly on small animals such as rabbits and voles. Other European wildcats look very similar.

The big cats

Large, wild cats, such as lions, pumas, tigers, leopards and cheetahs are usually called the "big cats."

Lions live in family groups called prides. There can be as many as thirty lions in a pride. Lions sometimes hunt alone like other cats, but often they hunt as a team. They approach their prey – perhaps a herd of wildebeeste – in a line. The lions at each end of the line loop round to surround the wildebeeste, driving them back toward the other lions, lying in wait.

The cheetah is said to be the fastest animal on Earth. It can touch 70 mph (113 km/h) but only for a minute or so. If it cannot bring down its prey quickly, it has to give up, panting with exhaustion.

The Asian tiger is the biggest cat of them all. This magnificent animal has claws that can measure a razor-sharp 4 in (10 cm) in length.

▽ Lions live in open country and scrublands in Africa and parts of India. They are the only cats to hunt in teams. All others are lone hunters. Lions spend much of their time not hunting, but sleeping in the shade or lazily lolling in the branches of trees.

10

◁ A cheetah running at top speed after its prey. Unlike other cats, cheetahs rarely climb trees, preferring to stay at ground level.

11

Domestic cats

△ Here you see four stages in the fall of a cat. See how it twists round to land on its feet.

Domestic cats are those we keep in our homes as pets. Unlike dogs, which vary enormously in build, pet cats are all roughly the same size and shape.

The picture on the right shows you the bones which make up a cat's skeleton. These bones are light in weight and, together with strong muscles, make cats very agile animals, well suited for the hunting life. Even the tamest pet cat likes to go out looking for a mouse when it gets the chance. Powerful leg muscles allow a cat to jump high in the air or race up a tree after prey or to escape an enemy, such as a fierce dog.

Cats have very supple spines that bend easily. This enables cats to twist and turn in mid-air, giving them a good chance of landing on their feet if they fall from a tree or a fence. The same suppleness lets them squeeze through narrow gaps.

12

The neck is very flexible. It allows the cat to look directly behind.

The spine bends easily, so the cat can squeeze through narrow spaces and turn around in mid-air.

The tail is an extension of the spine. It helps the cat to balance.

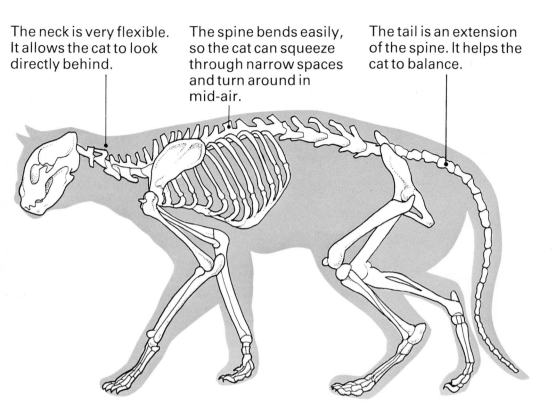

▷ This cat is arching its back into a tall curve to make itself look larger. The fur stands on end, too, making the cat look still bigger. Perhaps it will frighten off the curious dog!

Whiskers, claws and tails

△ Cats' whiskers are used as delicate feelers. Never pull them – you will hurt the animal.

Cats' whiskers are very sensitive and are used as feelers. A nerve cell at the base of each whisker sends a message to the brain if the whisker brushes against something or even if there is a sudden change in air pressure.

The curved claws of a cat help it to grip when climbing and are used as a deadly weapon to slash at enemies or prey, such as a bird. The claws can also be drawn back into the paws. This allows the cat to move silently while out hunting. If the claws were out all the time, they would make a giveaway "click-click" on hard surfaces and they would get blunt very quickly.

A cat's tail is an extension of its backbone. It helps the cat balance when climbing, jumping or walking along narrow branches or high walls. It is not absolutely essential for this though, otherwise the tailless Manx cat would have died out years ago!

▷ This cat's upright tail helps its balance on a narrow branch. Tails also give an idea of the cat's feelings. An upright tail is a form of greeting. A waving tail is a sign that the cat is angry.

▽ This diagram shows how a cat's claw moves in and out of its paw.

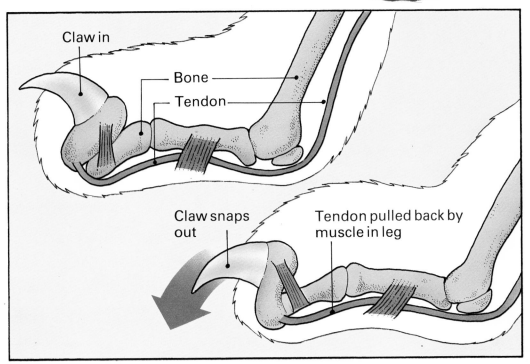

Claw in

Bone

Tendon

Claw snaps out

Tendon pulled back by muscle in leg

15

Seeing in the dark

In bright light the pupil closes to a slit.

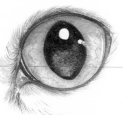

In dim light the pupil gets bigger to let more light in.

The human eye has a round pupil, unlike the slit shape of a cat's pupil.

△ In a bright light the pupil of the cat's eye closes to a narrow slit. In the dark the pupil opens fully to let in as much light as possible.

Cats are animals which hunt mainly at night. They have senses which are suited for the job. They can see in dim conditions much better than we can. Look at a cat's eyes in a bright light and you will see that the pupils are closed to a narrow slit. In the dark, they enlarge to become big and round. This lets in as much light as possible.

At the back of a cat's eye is a special layer called the tapetum. This layer

reflects light rather like a mirror. It gives the light-sensitive cells in the eye a second chance to pick up the faintest rays of light.

△ This cat makes a fine night-hunter, thanks to its keen eyesight and acute hearing.

In total darkness where there is no light at all – in a cellar perhaps – a cat can obviously see nothing. But it has sensitive hearing and can listen to noises too high pitched or faint for us to hear. Its whiskers, too, help it to feel its way to avoid stumbling into things.

Shorthair cats

△ The Siamese probably came from Siam, now Thailand. The darker areas on the head, ears, legs and tail are called points. These come in various colors, including blue, lilac, chocolate and seal-brown.

There are many breeds of domestic cat, but they can all be divided into two main groups, longhairs and shorthairs.

The tabby is probably the most common shorthair cat. You can see one at the beginning of this book. All tabbies have similar zig-zag or mackerel markings on their fur. Tabbies come in three colors, brown, red or silver.

Foreign shorthairs, such as the Siamese and Burmese, are slimmer

than the stocky tabby. They have pointed ears and slanting, oriental eyes. Siamese are born white all over. As they grow up, the fur on their feet, tail, ears and around the mouth darkens to one of several colors.

The only good place to see a wide variety of pure-breed cats is at an exhibition or show. Most of the cats near your home are likely to be mongrels, the result of mating between various breeds.

△ An Abyssinian kitten, hungry for supper! All cats' tongues are covered with tiny rough lumps called papillae. These help a cat groom itself. They act like a brush, pulling out loose hairs. They also help scrape bones clean of all meat.

Longhair cats

Longhair cats were first bred from the silky-furred Angora cat of Turkey and breeds from Persia. There are now many longhair breeds, but they all have features in common.

Longhairs have a different build to shorthairs. They have a sturdy body (called cobby by cat breeders) with short legs. Their head is broad with a short nose. The Himalayan, like the one shown here, has points like a Siamese, but with long flowing hair. There is also a longhair breed with tabby markings.

Black longhairs are often born a burnt-brown color. As they get older, the coat turns to jet-black.

All longhairs need lots of grooming. Few manage to keep their fur silky smooth without a daily brush and comb from their owner. For cat shows, a grooming trick is to polish the fur to a gleaming sheen with velvet or silk!

▽ The Himalayan cat has a pale coat, darkening at the points of its body. Kittens are born off-white, the colors growing through a few days later.

▷ Black longhairs have
deep orange or copper
colored eyes. Like other
longhairs, they have a
thick ruff of fur around
the face.

21

Unusual cats

△ Odd-eye cats are born with two blue eyes. One eye changes slowly to orange during the two or three months after birth.

The Isle of Man in the Irish Sea is the home of a cat without a tail – the Manx cat. There are several legends about how the cat lost its tail. One of them tells how the cat was the last to board Noah's ark. It got on just as Noah was shutting the door. Its tail was trapped and was left behind.

Apart from its lack of tail, the Manx has another claim to fame. Its back legs are longer than its front legs. This gives it a curious hopping sort of walk.

Another unusual cat is the Sphinx, from Canada, which has no hair. In fact, it does have a fine covering of soft down, but this is almost invisible.

A strange-looking, but beautiful, cat is the odd-eyed white. This is the result of breeding between orange- and blue-eyed parents. Some of the kittens have odd-colored eyes. Like other blue-eyed whites, they are often deaf on the blue-eyed side.

▷ Most cats dislike water, although they can swim. The Turkish Van shown here is an exception – it loves to go in the water.

▽ This Manx has no tail at all and is known as a rumpy. If the tail bones can be felt, it is called a riser. A stumpy has a short tail, while a longy has a longer but not completely full-length tail.

23

Kittens

When a kitten is born, it is blind and completely helpless. It burrows up to its mother's belly to suckle milk from her. For the first few weeks this is all the food it needs.

When it is about nine days old, the kitten's eyes begin to open, but it cannot see well for several more days.

At two to three weeks, the kitten's teeth begin to develop. It can now stand and might be taking its first rather wobbly steps.

By the time it is six weeks old, a kitten will play with anything it finds. Kittens are naturally very playful and this is one way they learn their hunting skills. The mother is always nearby though, ready to pick it up by the scruff of its neck if it is too naughty or strays too far. She washes and cleans her kittens and may cradle a frightened kitten in her paws, licking it all over to calm it.

24

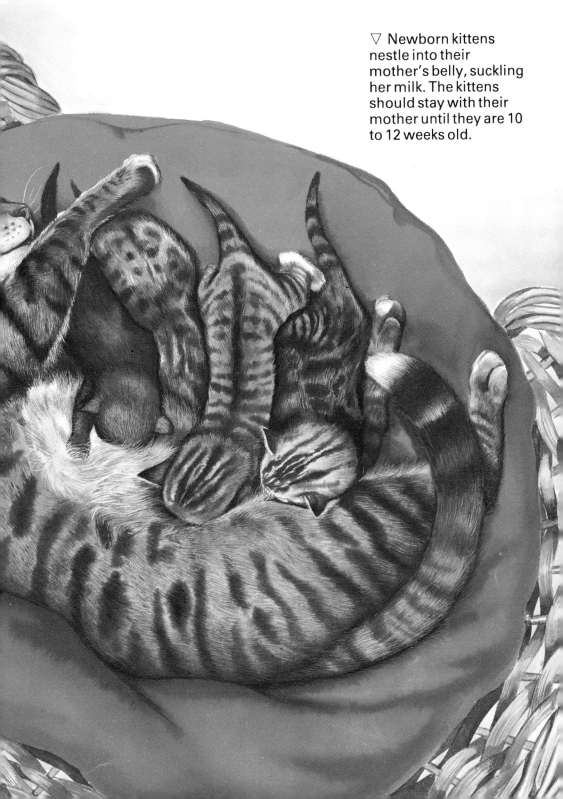

▽ Newborn kittens nestle into their mother's belly, suckling her milk. The kittens should stay with their mother until they are 10 to 12 weeks old.

Growing up

△ This mother cat picks up her kittens by the scruff of the neck but you should not do this. Support the kitten with both hands to lift it. Turn the cat toward your body so that it can cling to your clothes for extra support.

Kittens can start to eat solid food in addition to their mother's milk from four weeks old. By six weeks a kitten should no longer need its mother's milk. Teaching a kitten to change from milk to solid food is called weaning. Weaning kittens do best on four small meals a day, reducing to two meals after six months.

Cats use their claws for climbing, hunting and to defend themselves, so

Cat litter tray

Solid food

Water

Cornish Rex kitten

Box lined with newspapers and a rug

Silver paper ball

Ping pong ball

they have to be kept in good condition. They need to sharpen their claws and will scratch anything in the house – including armchairs and table legs. A scratching post is a good solution to this problem. Use an 18 in (45 cm) length of wood and screw it firmly to a wooden base. Cover the post with a length of old carpet, firmly nailed on. The post should keep your kitten's claws away from the furniture.

△ Apart from a supply of food and fresh water, you will need a litter tray for your kitten until it is housetrained. A comfortable bed should be put in a warm place. Plenty of simple toys should also be provided.

Caring for your cat

△ Cats are independent creatures, so it is a good idea to have a cat flap like this put in the back door. The cat can then come and go as it pleases.

Cats are fussy eaters, but try to give yours a varied diet. Good canned foods will give all the nourishment a cat needs. You can also give raw chopped meat or boiled fish, mixed with bread. Make sure there are no bones in the fish – your cat could choke on one.

Always have fresh water in a bowl. Cats love milk, but do not need it as part of their regular diet. In fact, too much milk will usually make a cat fat.

Cats are normally healthy animals, but check with a vet if yours looks ill or off-color.

Cats often live for 12–15 years, and some live longer than this – the world record is 34 years old. Any cat over ten will show signs of old age. It moves more slowly, the fur loses its sheen, the nose becomes dry and the eyes lose their color.

When your cat gets old, treat it gently and keep it warm and comfy.

▷ If you take your cat anywhere, you will need a pet carrier. For short journeys a strong box will do. For longer ones a carrier like this one, made of wicker, will be best.

▽ Cats like warmth and comfort. They love to sleep in front of a fire or bask in the sunshine. This cat has found a good spot – the warm hood of a parked car.

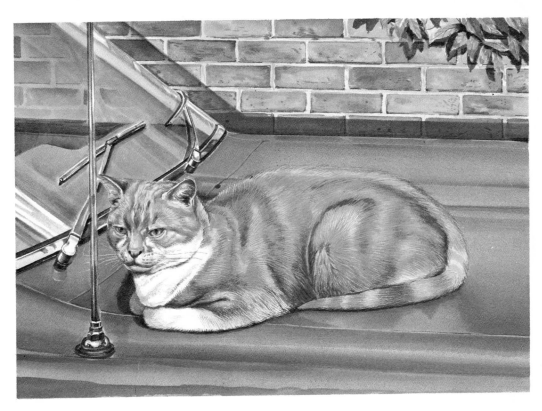

Glossary

Here is a list of some of the technical words used in this book.

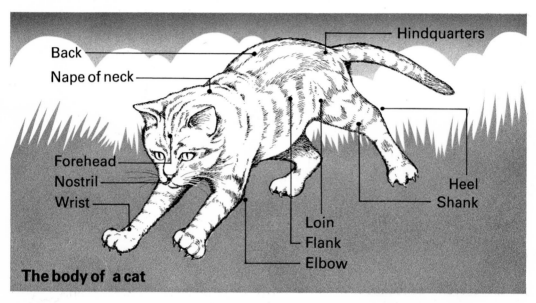

Back
Nape of neck
Hindquarters
Forehead
Nostril
Wrist
Heel
Shank
Loin
Flank
Elbow

The body of a cat

Breed
Type of cat, such as a Siamese or Abyssinian. If different breeds mate, the kittens have some of the features of each parent. They are called cross-breeds or mongrels. Two cats of the same breed will have pure-breed kittens. Ordinary cross-breeds make fine pets.

Dinictis
Ancestor of the cat, which lived about 36 million years ago.

Grooming
Keeping a cat's fur brushed, combed and clear of loose hair and dirt. All cats spend time grooming themselves, but many longhairs need brushing too.

Ice Age
Period in which glaciers advanced from the polar regions. There were several ice ages, the last ending about 10,000 years ago.

Mummy
Dead body which was preserved and wrapped in cloth by the Ancient Egyptians.

30

Cat facts

Here are some interesting facts about the world of cats.

Ancestors
The cat ancestor, *Dinictis*, was in turn descended from *Miacis*. This small meat-eater was the ancestor of a number of other animals too, including dogs, bears, raccoons and weasels.

Curiosity
"Curiosity killed the cat" is a very old saying, and can be all too true. A cat's interest in strange objects can result in its getting its head stuck in anything from a tin can to a teapot.

Home from the hunt
A cat coming home from a night hunt will sometimes (or often!) bring its owner a "present" – the dead body of a bird or a mouse. This is the natural instinct of a cat, bringing back food for its kittens.

Mirrors
Cats often stare for long periods at themselves in mirrors. The reflection looks like another cat, and sometimes they will make all sorts of aggressive actions, spitting and snarling at the stranger in the mirror.

Water
While few cats like having a swim, almost all are fascinated by the movement of water. They will splash away with their paws for fun and interest.

Independence
Cats are by nature very self-contained animals, unlike dogs who need constant attention and affection. Whilst any cats enjoys being made a fuss of, if it is not in the right mood, it will simply ignore any attempts you make to play with it.

Longest journey
Cats are renowned for covering incredible distances, especially when finding their home territory. In 1949 a ginger cat called Rusty walked all the way from Boston, Massachusetts, to Chicago, Illinois – a distance of 950 miles (1,530 km)!

The worth of a cat
In AD 935 the Welsh prince Hywel Dda decreed that a cat was worth one penny until its eyes opened and two-pence once it had caught a mouse.

First cat show
The first cat show ever held was in the glass-walled Crystal Palace, London, in 1871, when 170 cats were entered for the exhibition.

The smallest cat
Jasper, a dwarf tabby cat born in London in 1946, weighed only 3 lb 8 oz (1.58 kg) when full grown. He lived for 15 years.

Numbers
In Britain there are thought to be nearly five million cats. In the USA there are 34 million.

Index